humans and other animals

Tate Publishing

an A to Z
in sign language
and pictures

by Adam Broomberg and Oliver Chanarin

A is for arm

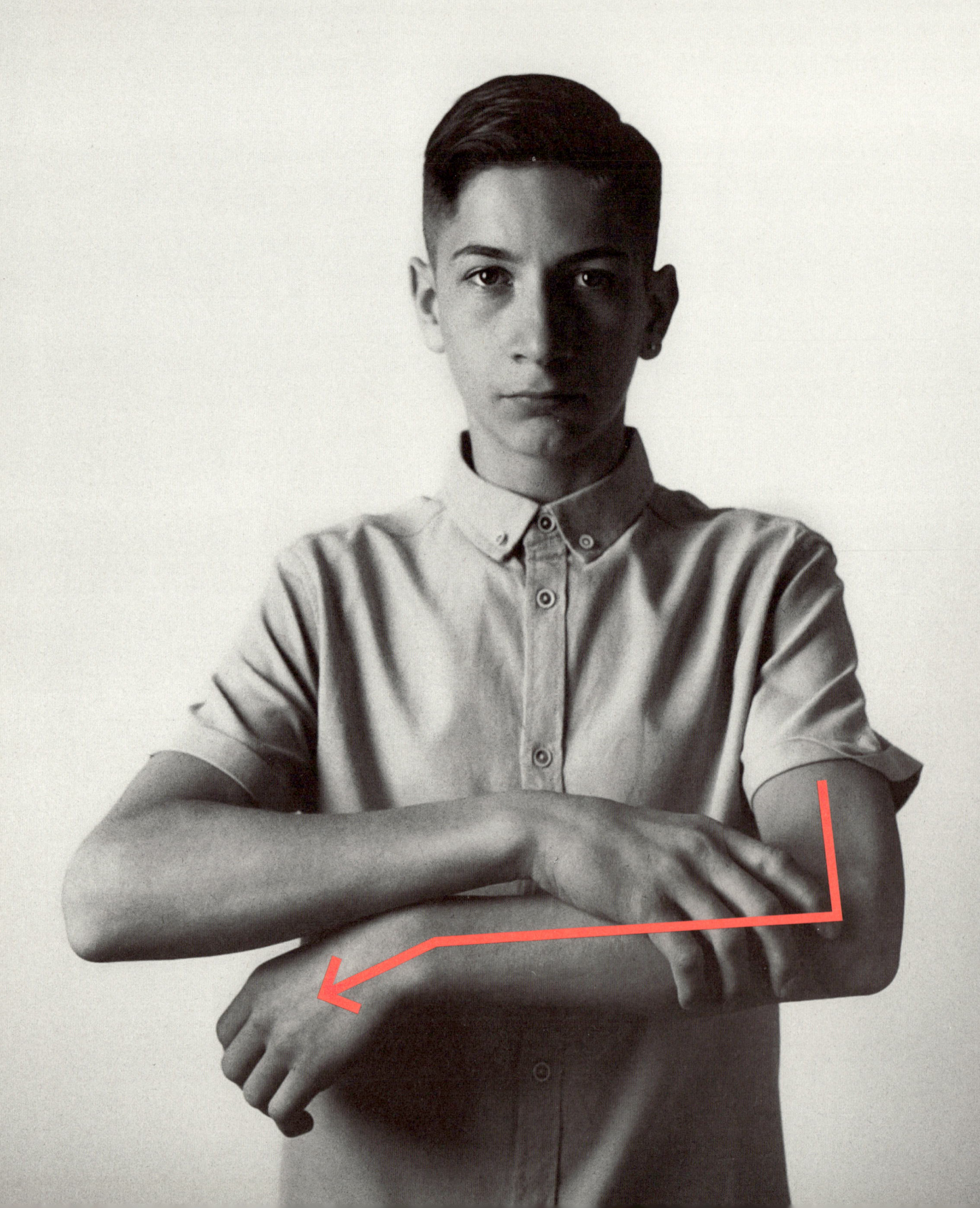

How many can you see?

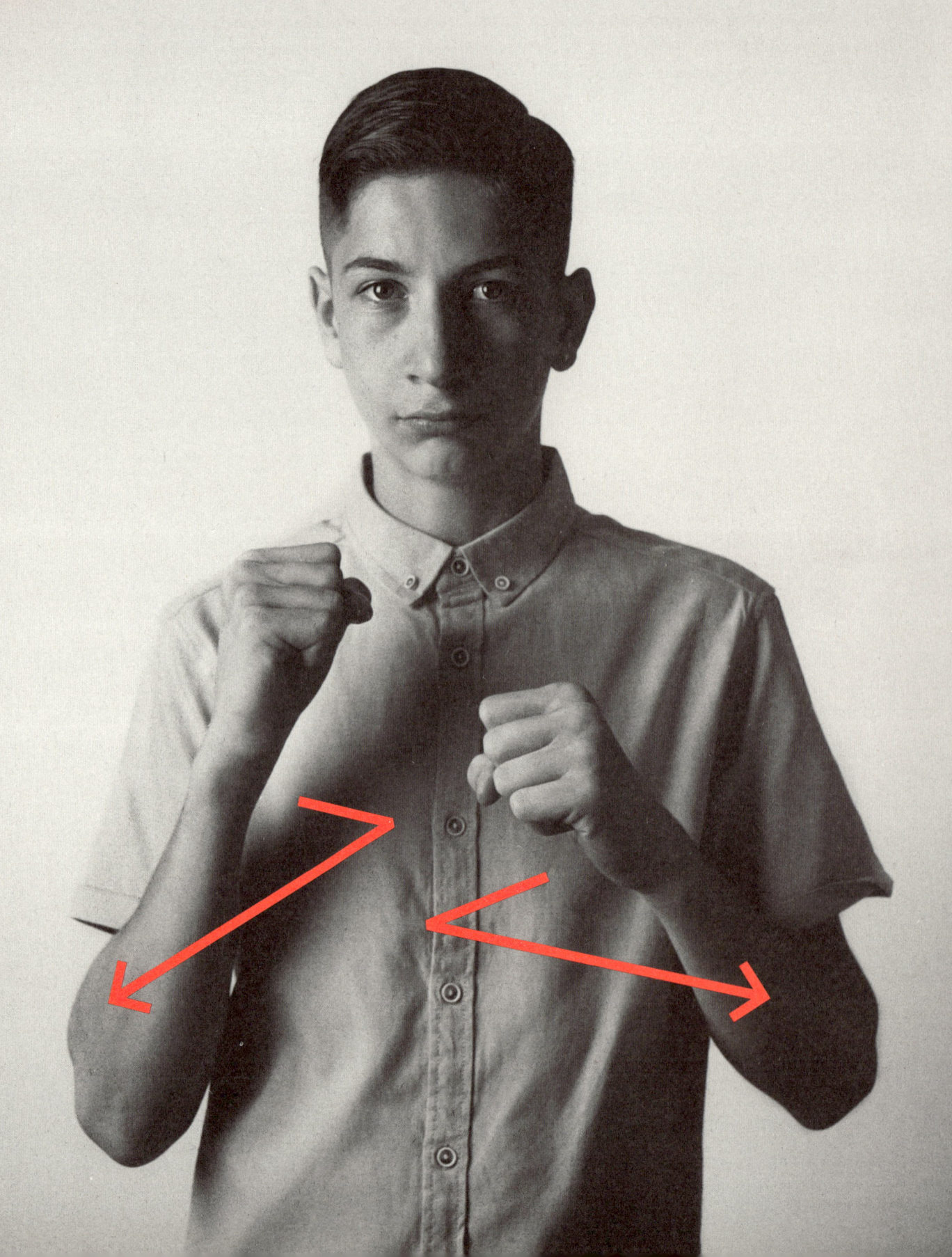

B is for BANG

between a tree

and a tree

C is for curious

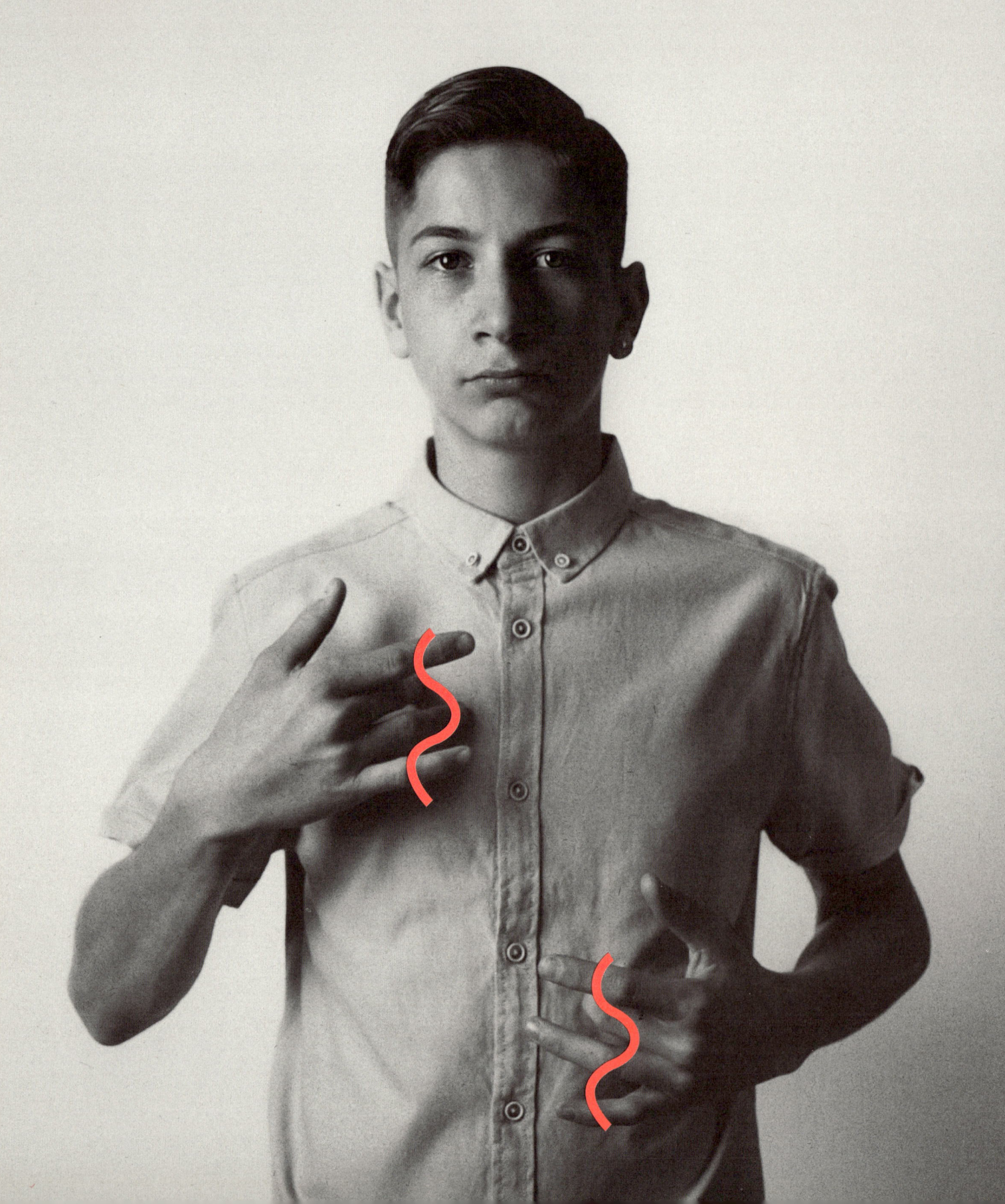

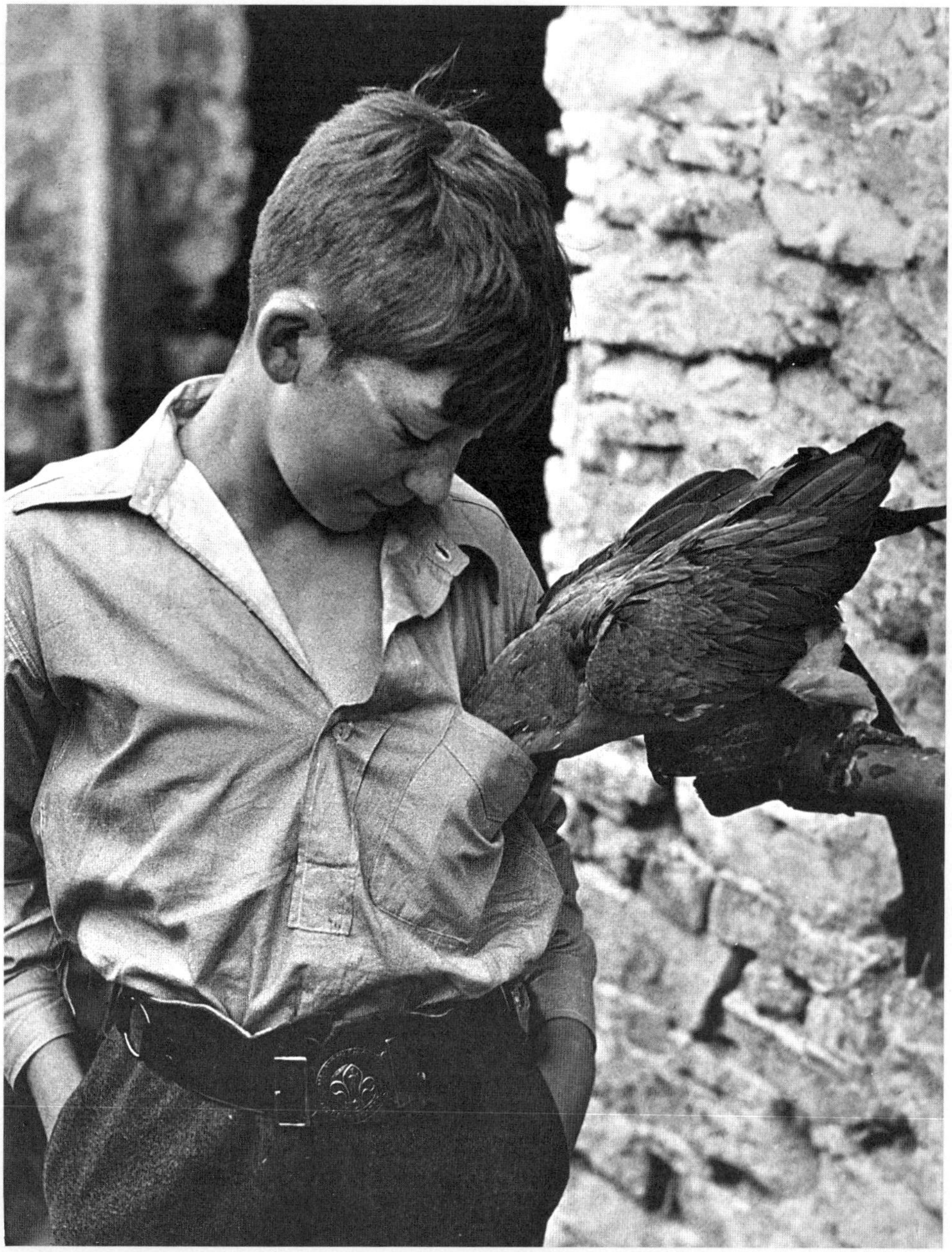

D is for dreaming

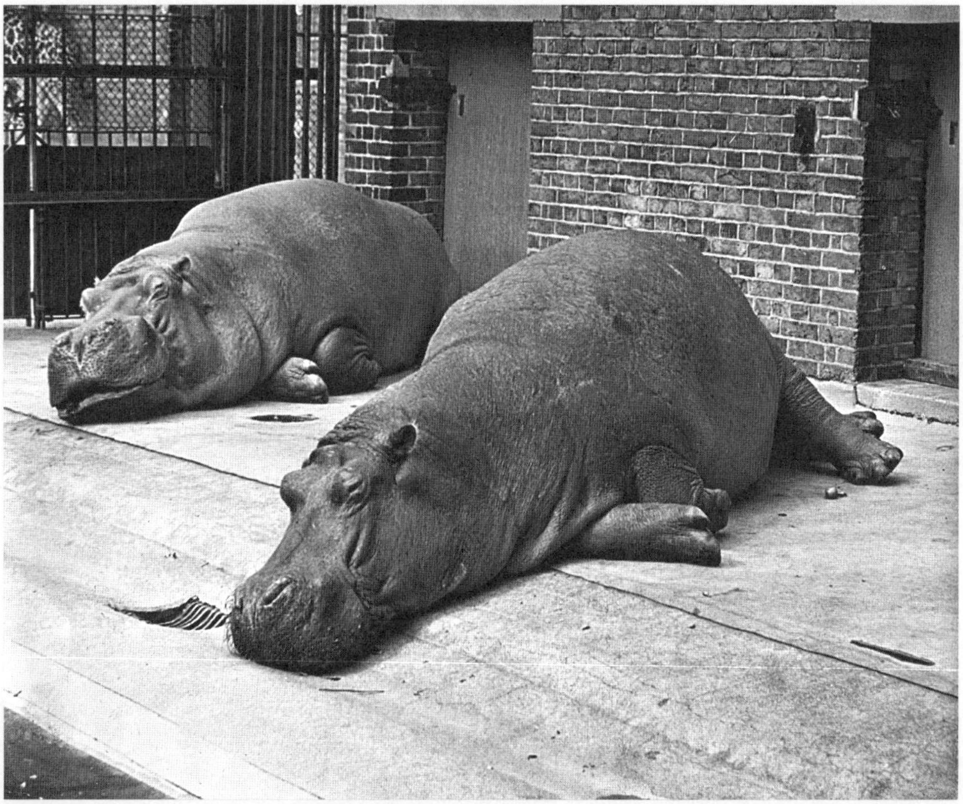

E is for escape

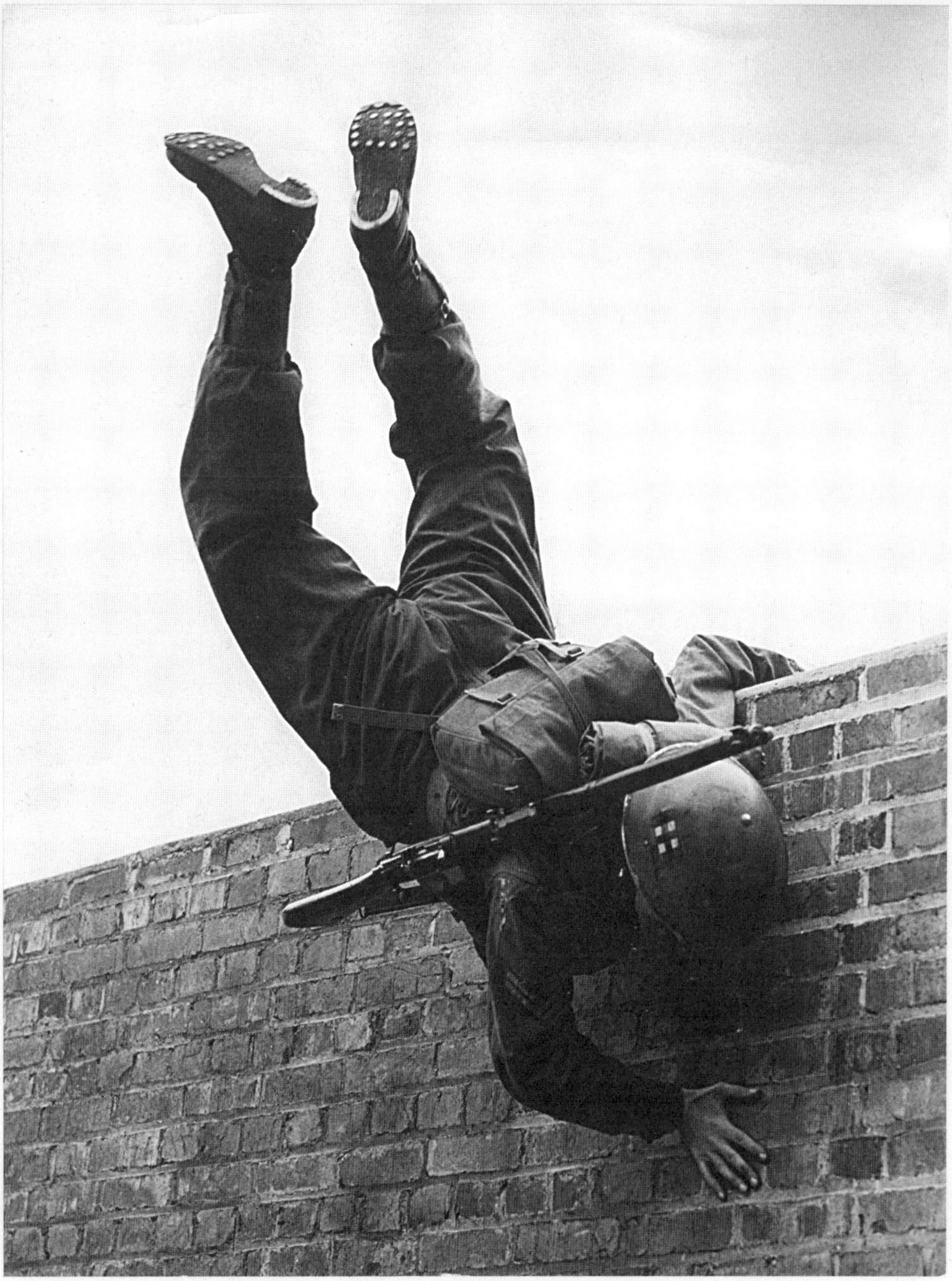

F is for fires

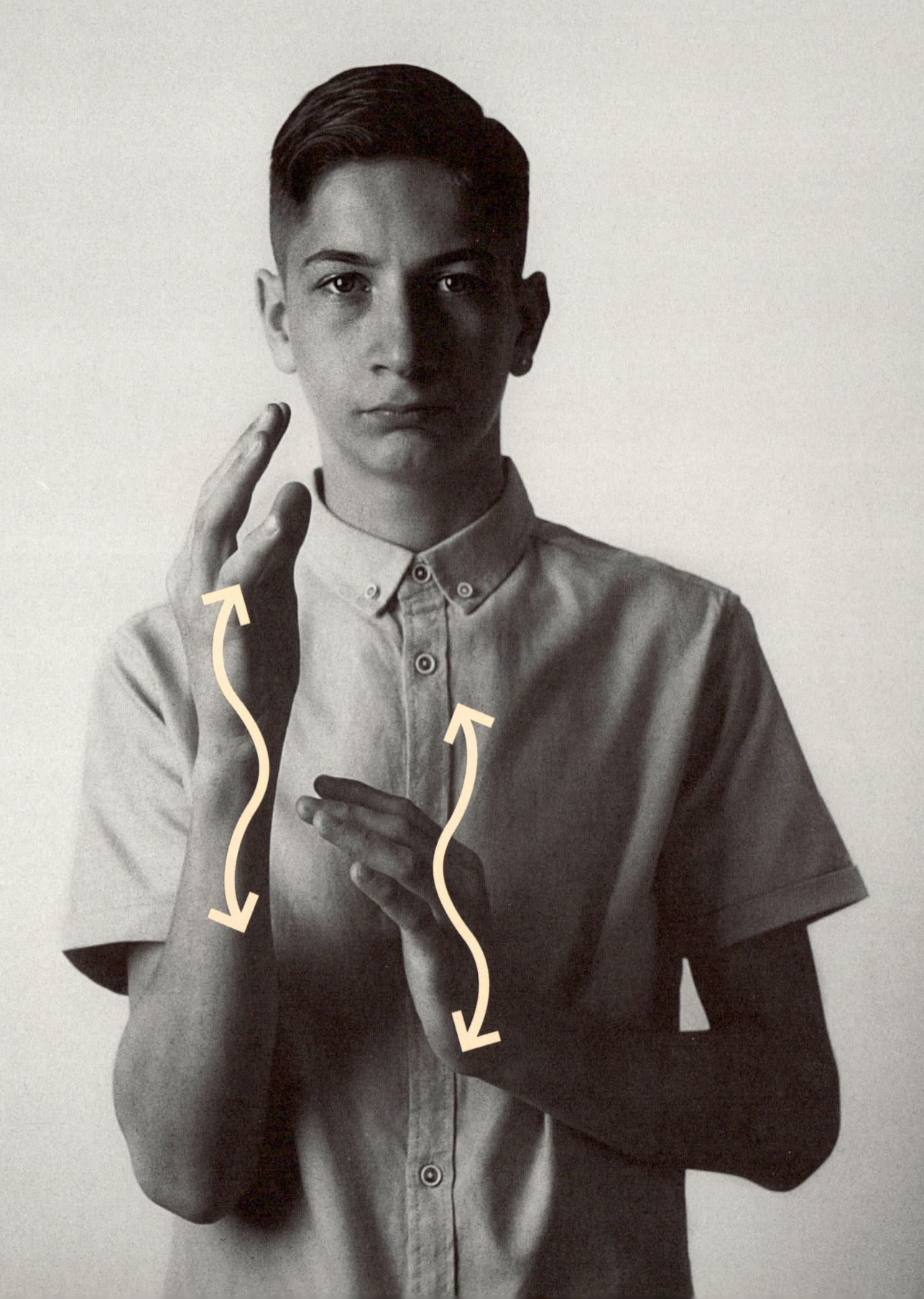

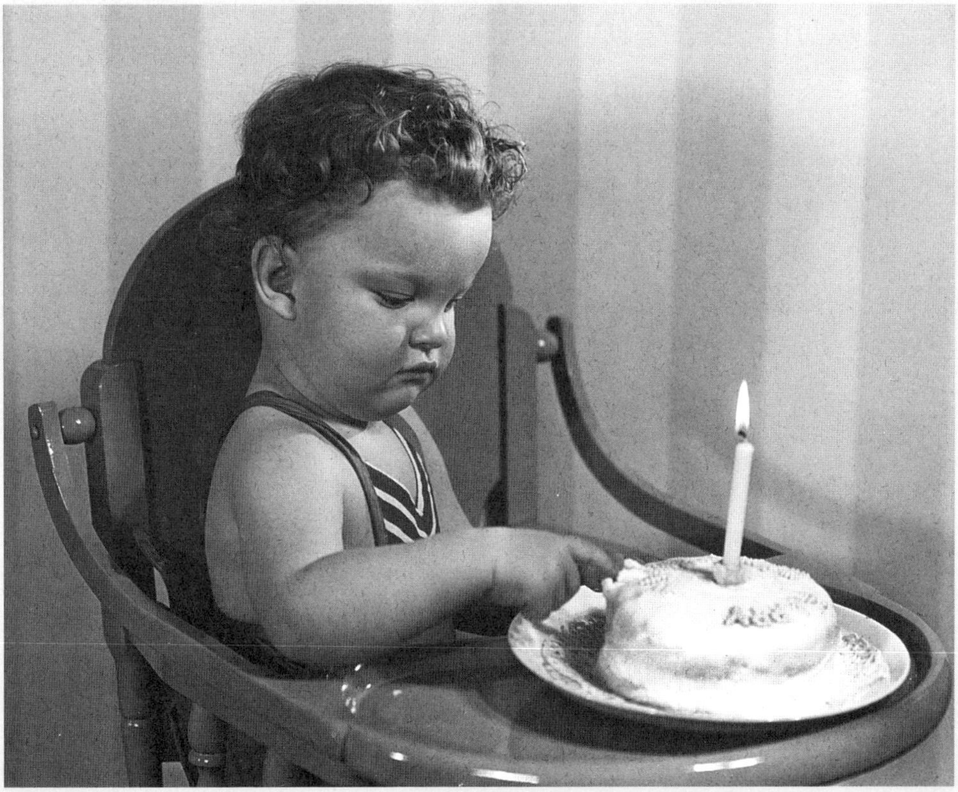

G is for gravity

What does that mean?

H is for heaven

Have you ever been?

I is for inhale

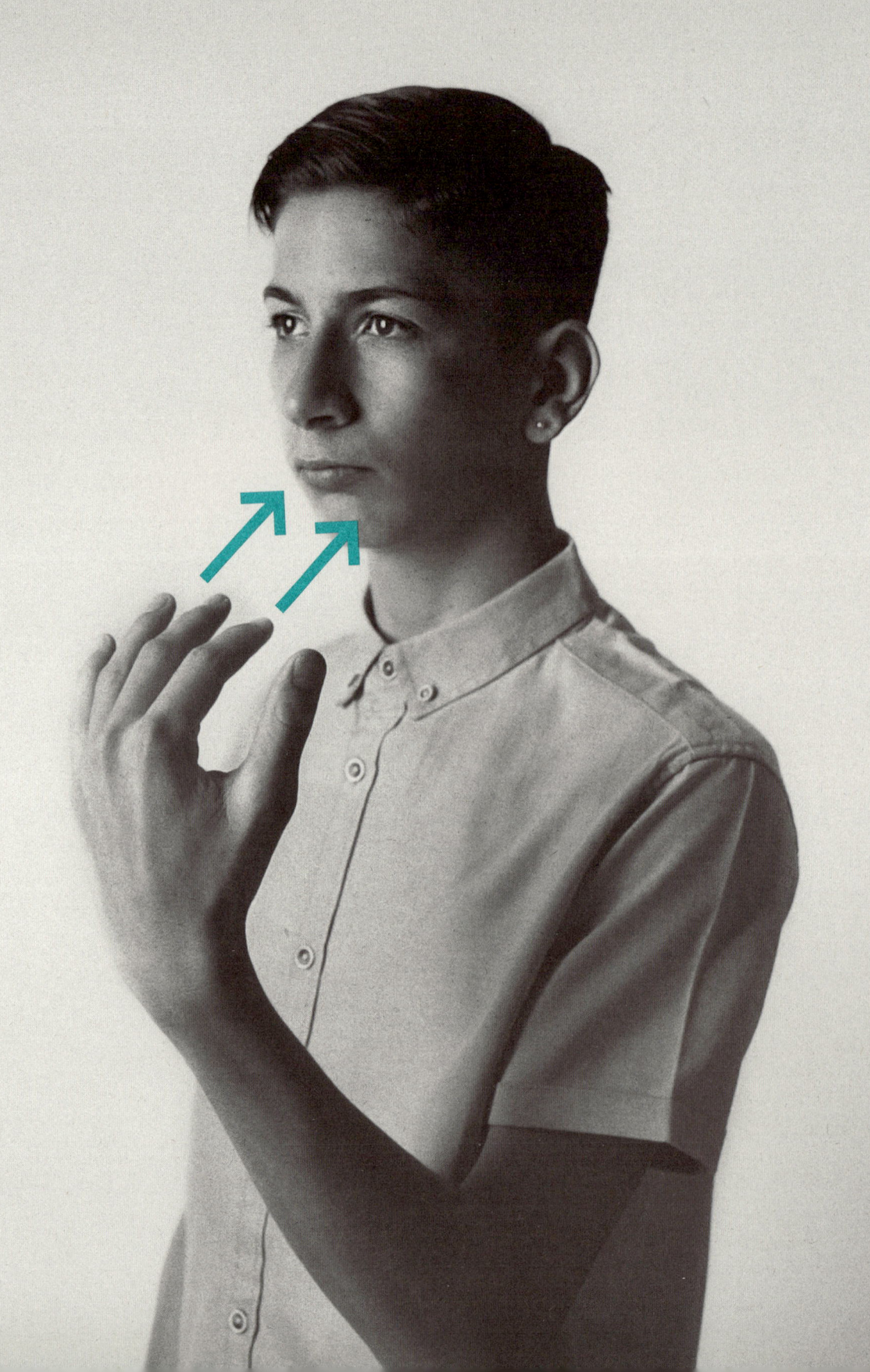

through the mouth
and the nose

J   is for jump

on the tips of your toes

K

is for kiss

on the lips with your beak

L

is for look

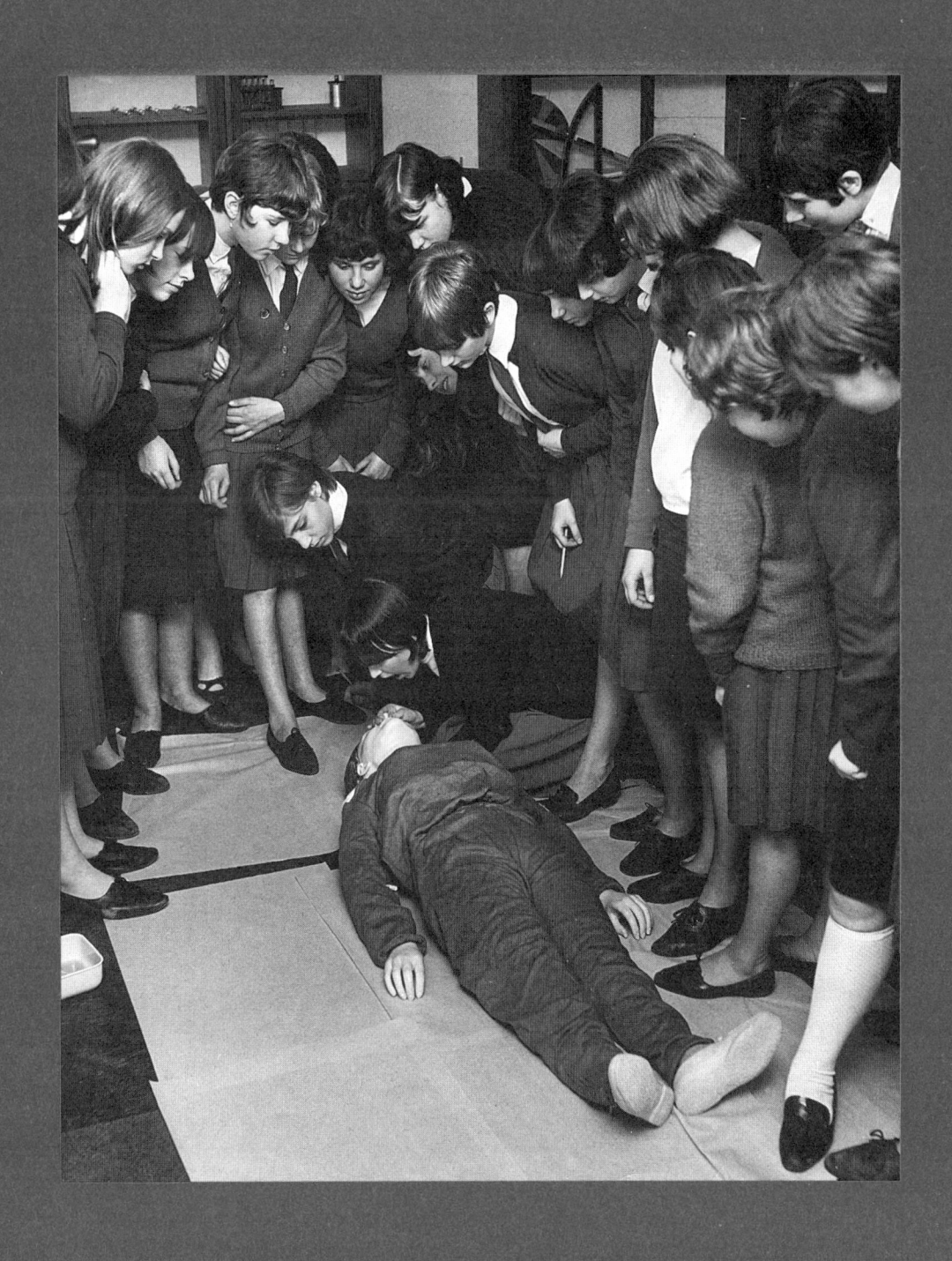

is she asleep?

M is for moon

seen from above

N is for nonsense

an elephant in love?

O is for over

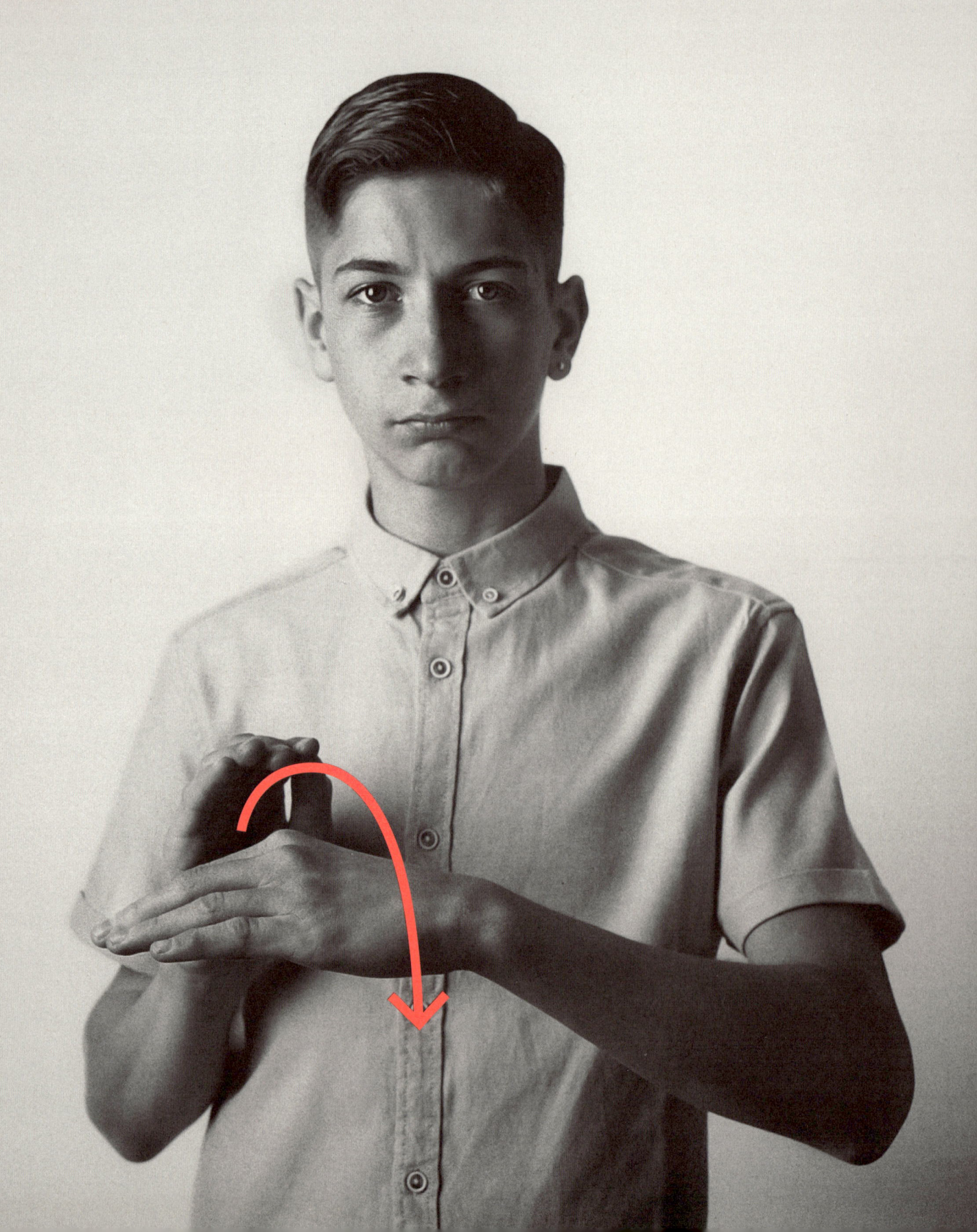

the back of

P is for painting

hung

Q is for quietly

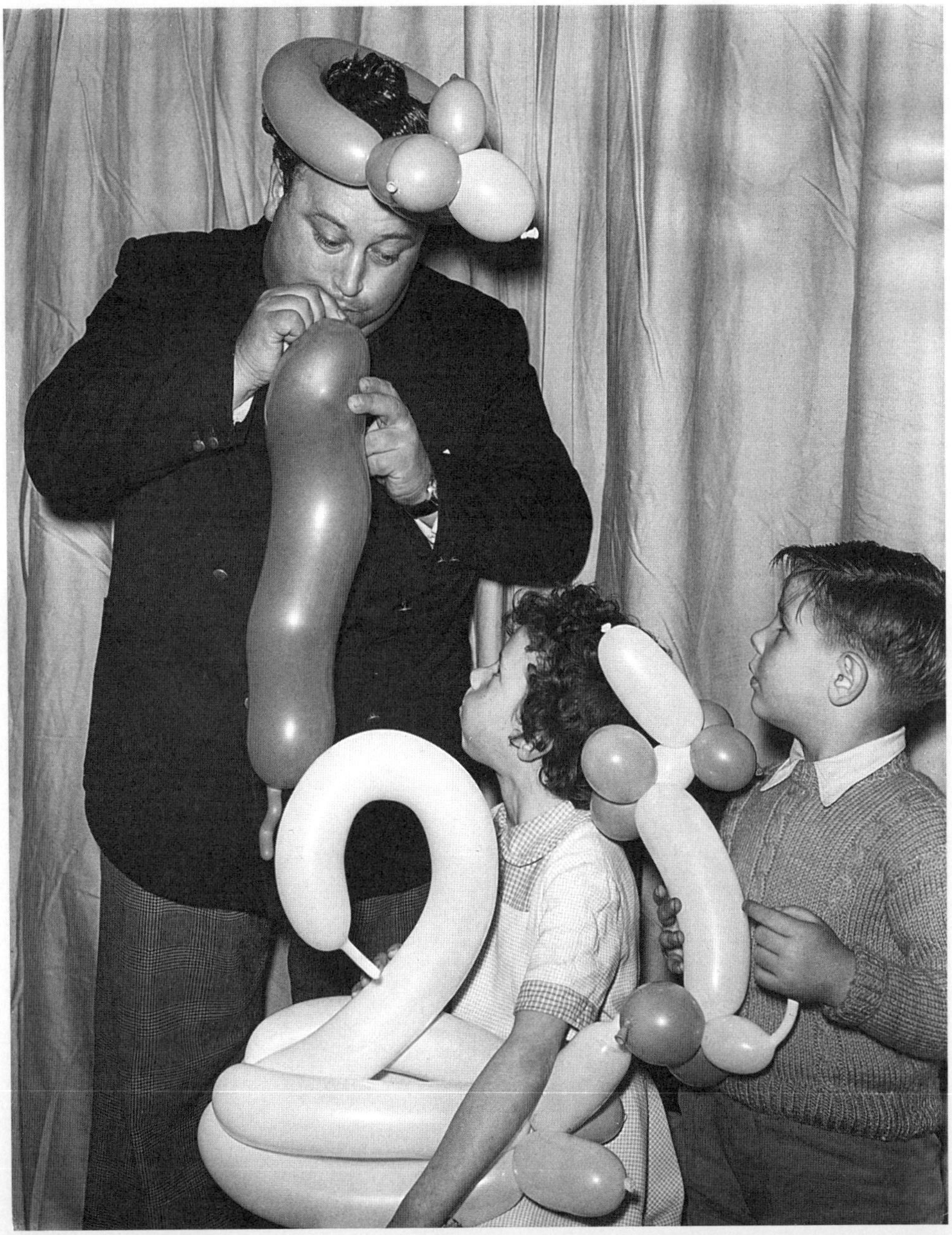

R

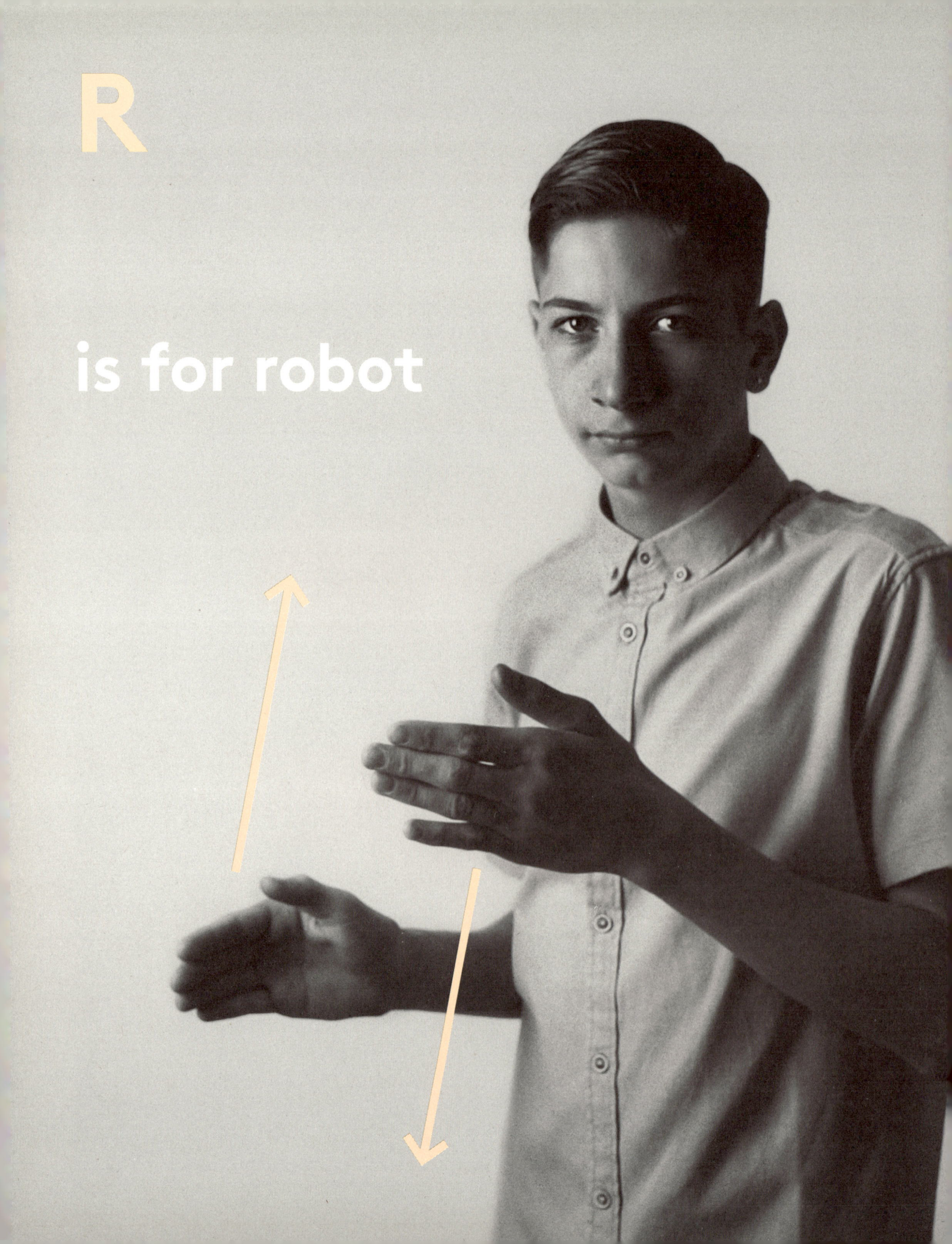

is for robot

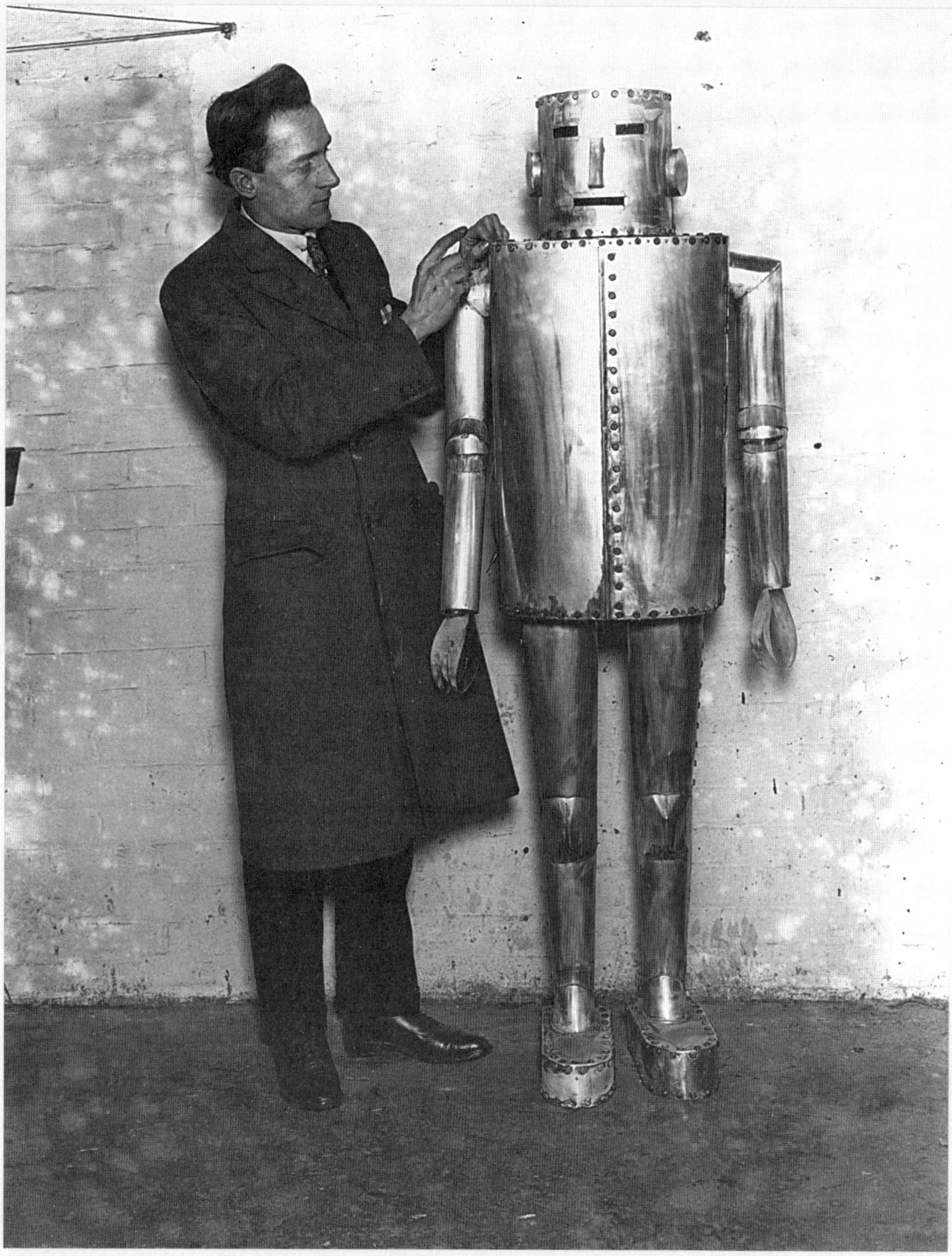

S is for shoes

glued to the ceiling

T

is for toes

how are they feeling?

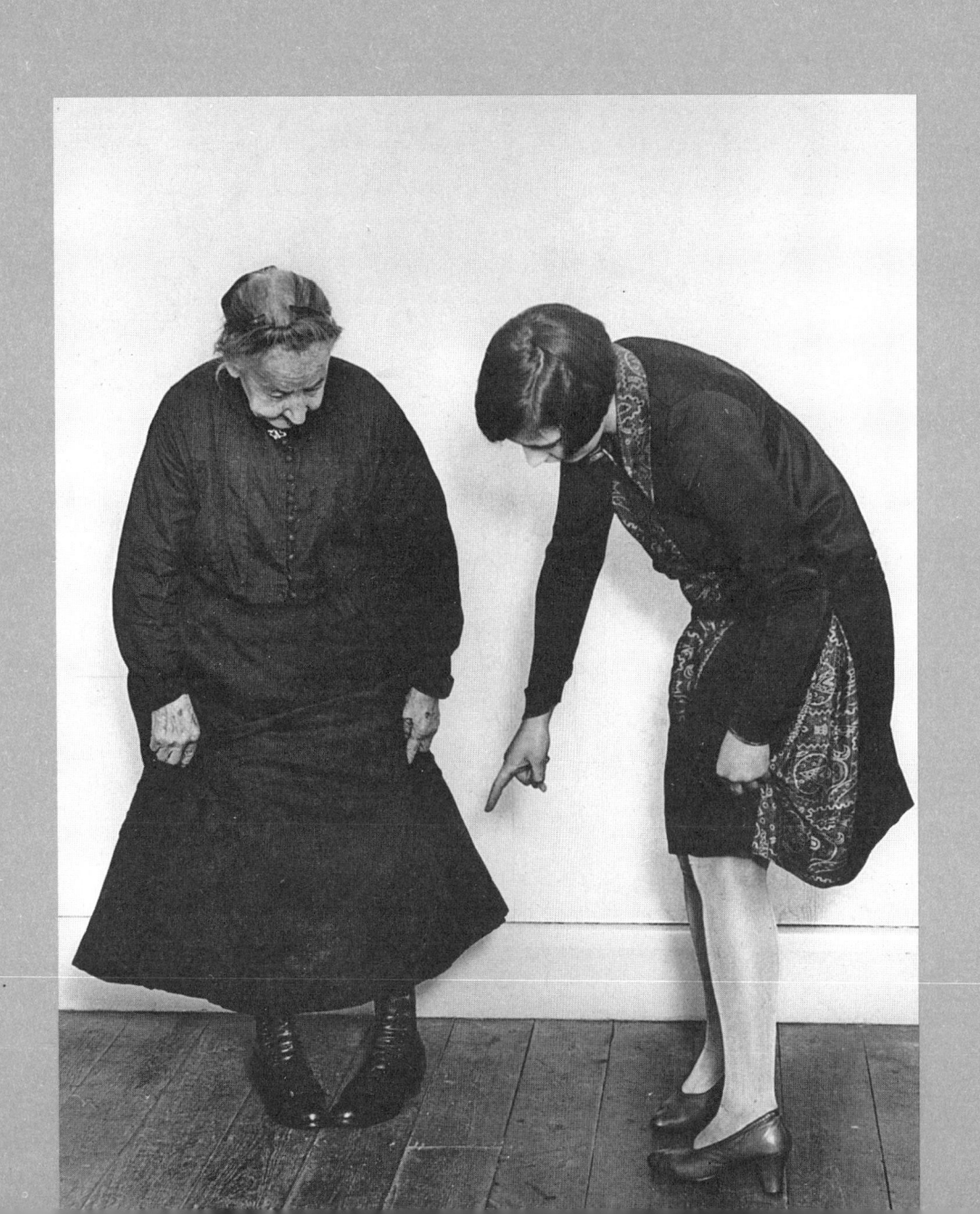

U

is for
unbelievable

can people fly?

V

is for visible

to the naked eye

W is for wish

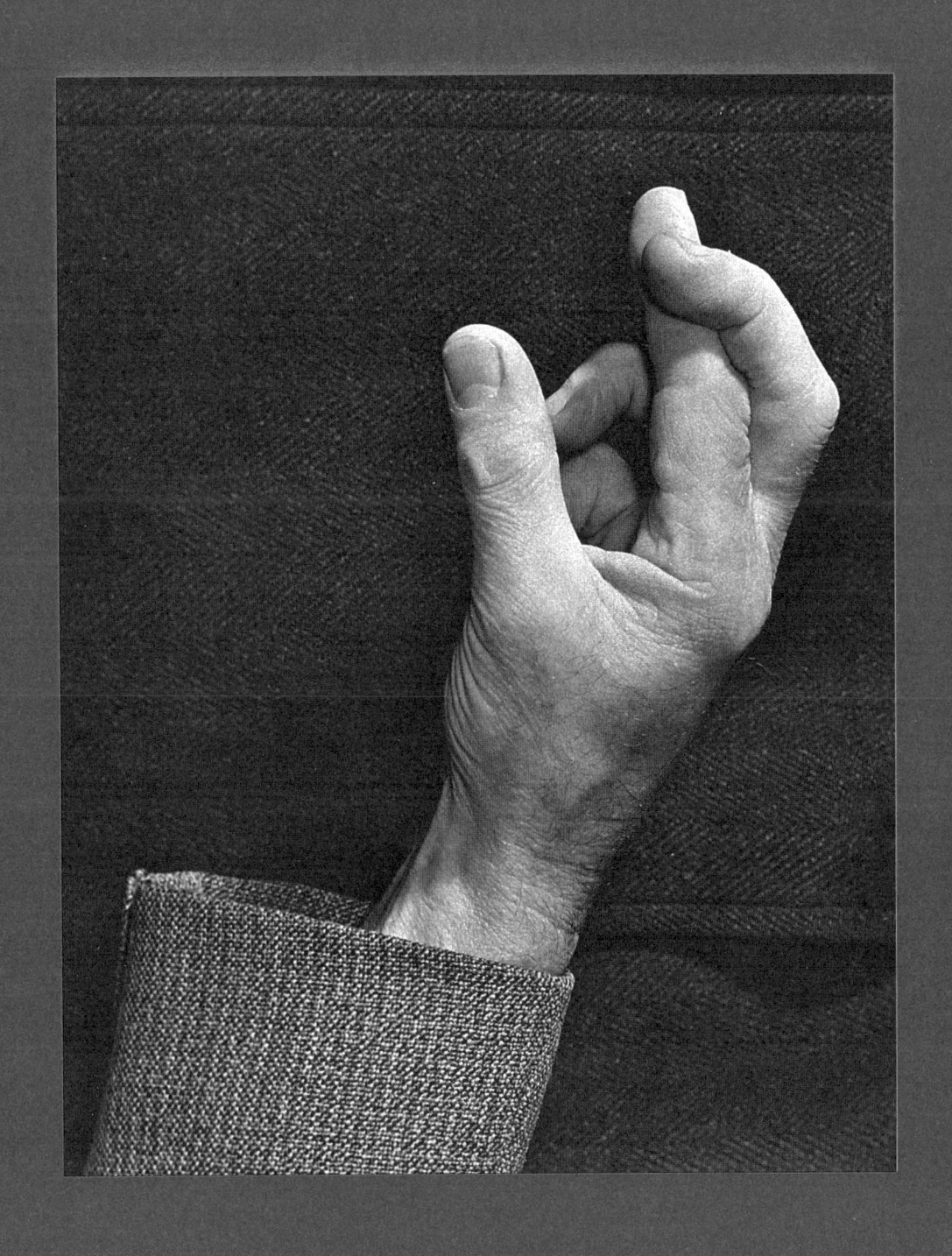

cross your toes too!

X is for X-ray

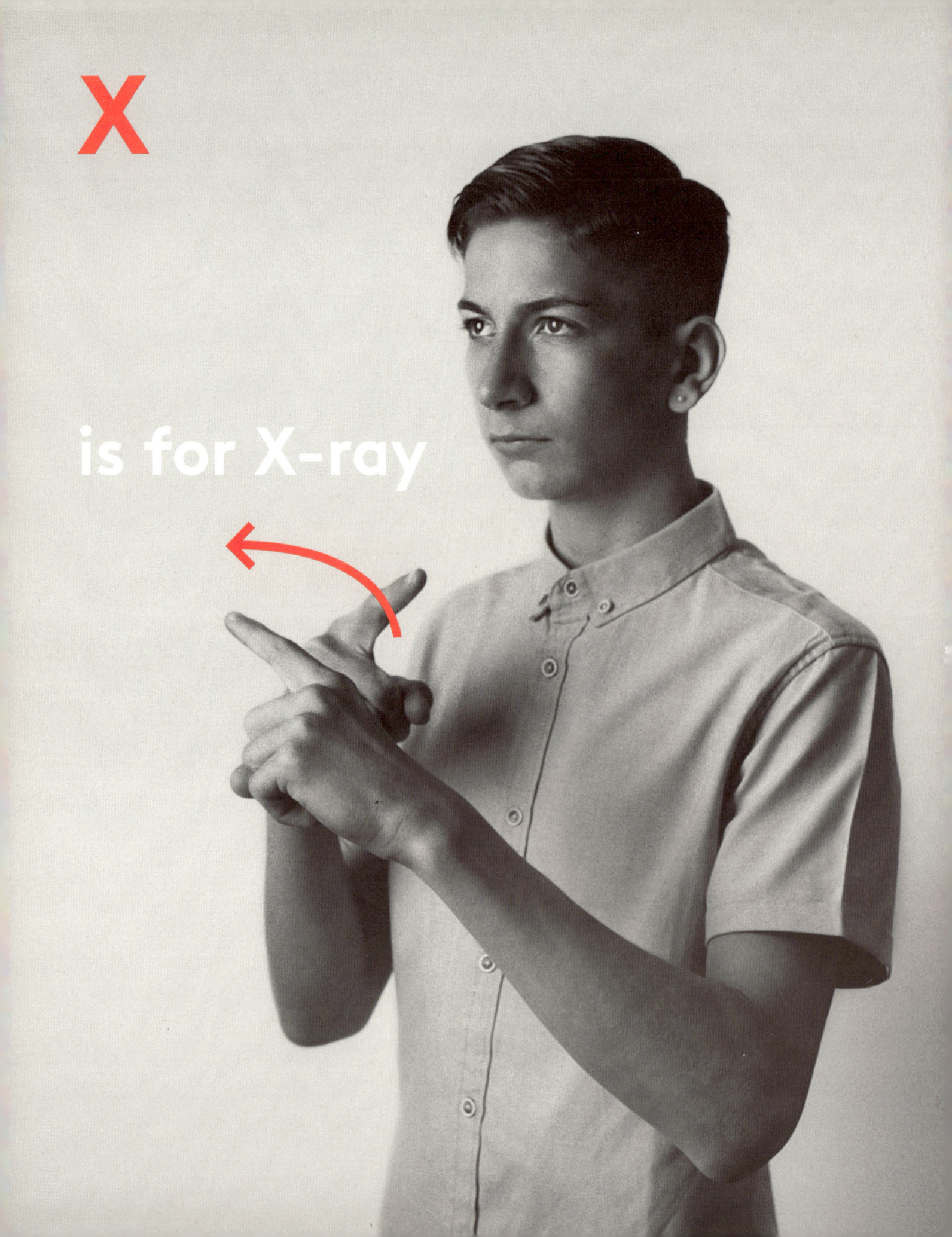

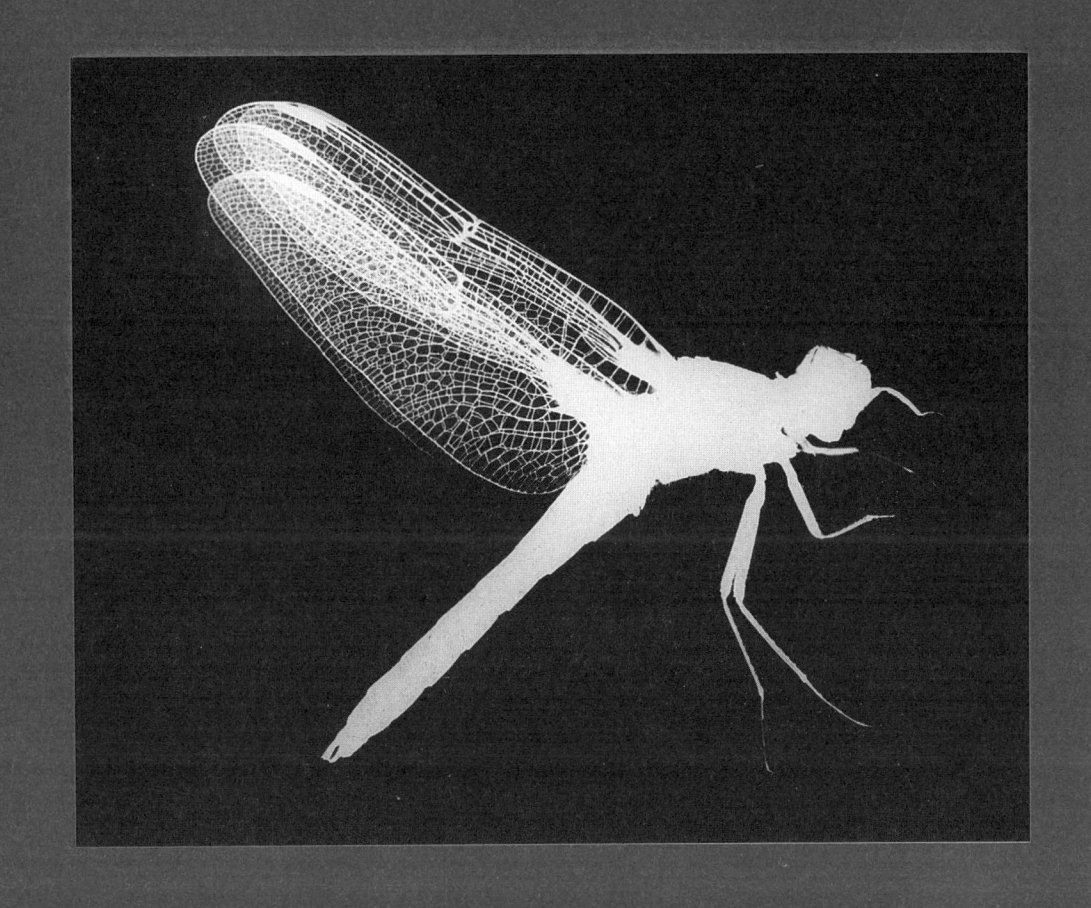

Can you see through?

Y is for yawn

sleep next to me

z

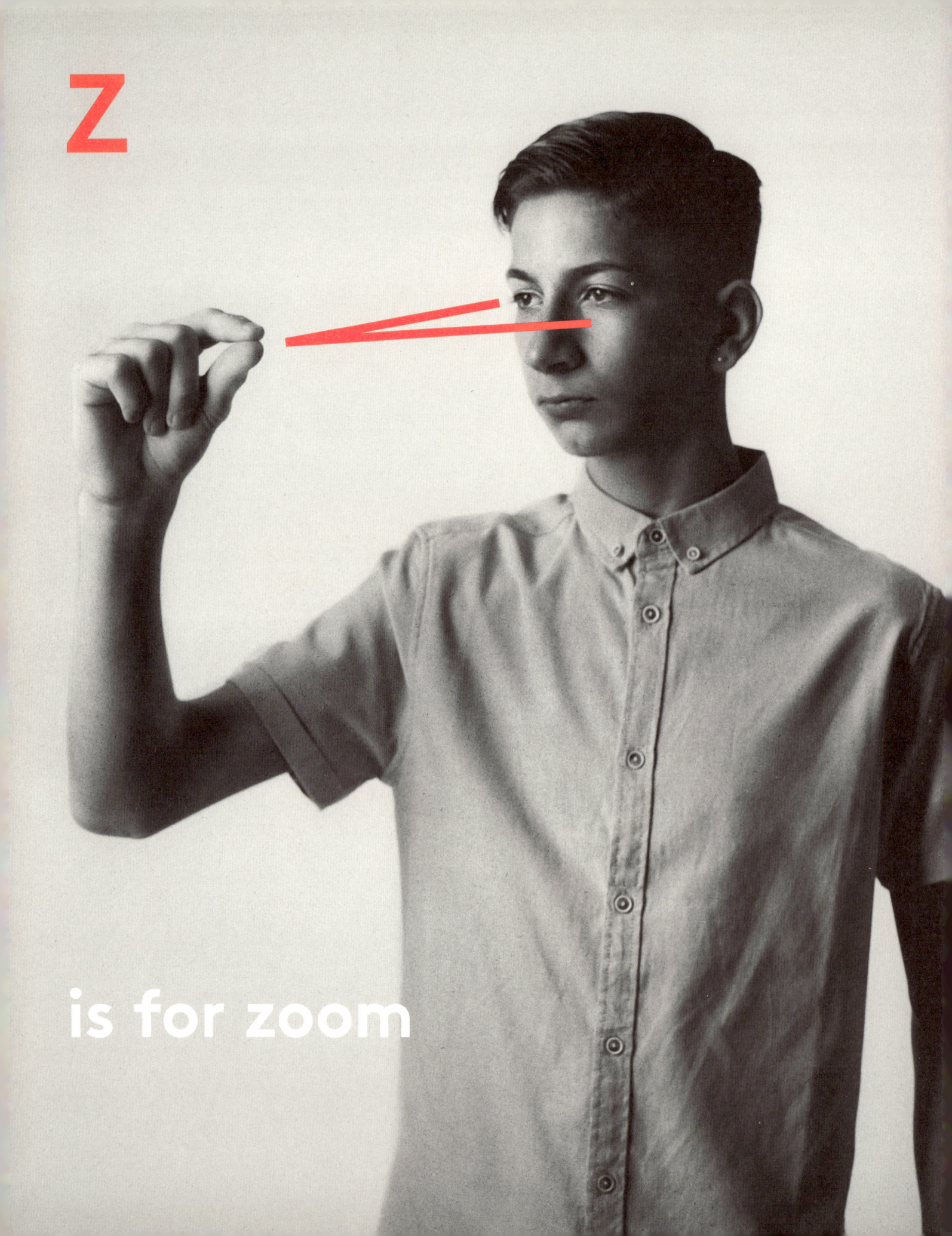

is for zoom

until there's nothing to see

zoom

zoom

zoom

zoom

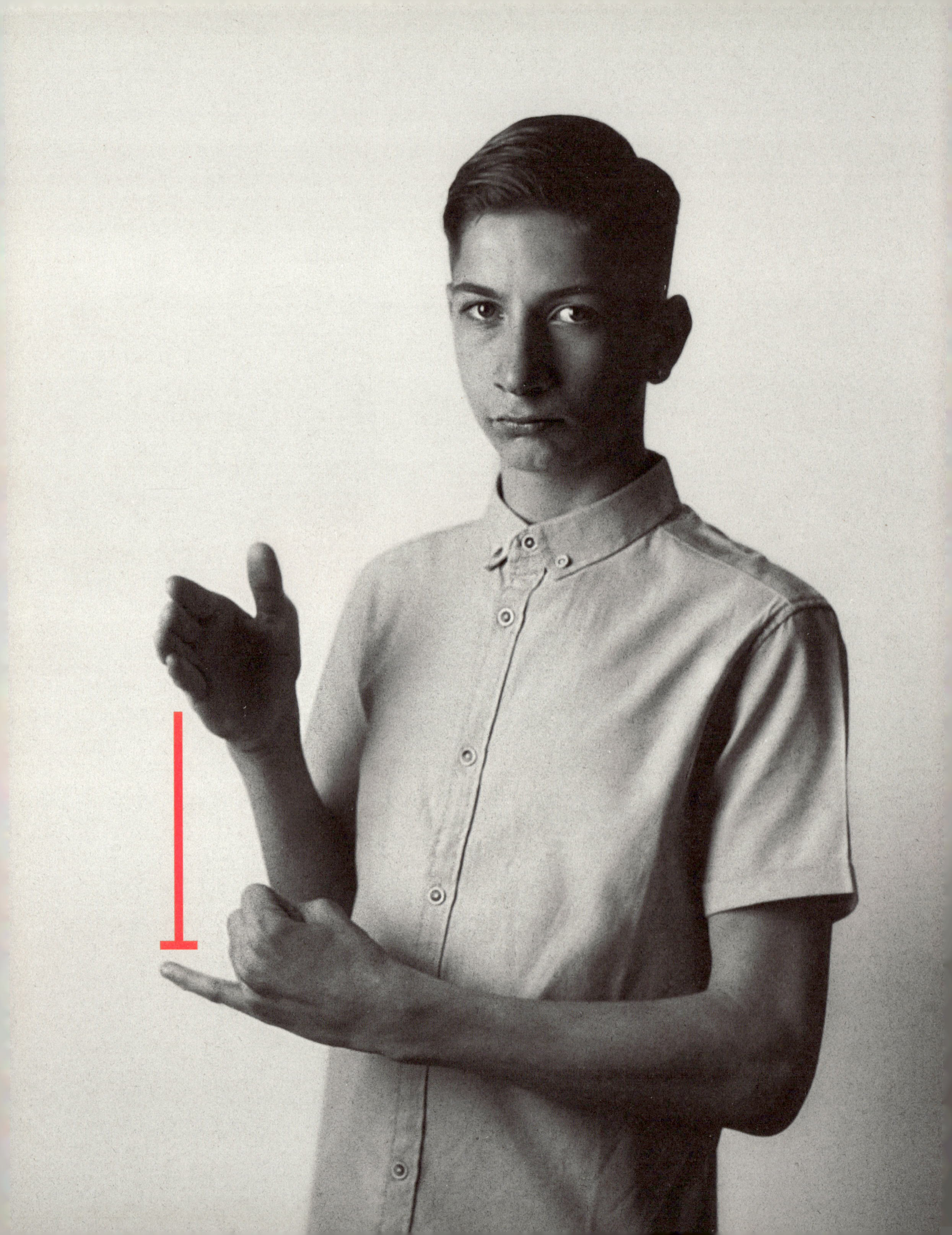

the end

Humans and Other Animals
by Adam Broomberg and Oliver Chanarin
with photographs from
the Getty Archive in London

Produced in collaboration with students and
staff at Frank Barnes School for Deaf Children

Designed by A Practice for Everyday Life
British sign language portraits by Broomberg & Chanarin
Archive photographs courtesy of Getty Images

Model: Connor Tompkins
Casting: Ilektra Stefanatou
Hair: Barry the barber
Photo Editors: Ilektra Stefanatou, Nicoletta Barbata
Colour reproduction by Evergreen, Hong Kong
Printed and bound in China by Toppan Leefung Printing Ltd

Thanks to Jamie Giles for inviting us to the Getty archive,
Charles Merullo, Jennifer Jeffrey, Sarah McDonald, Lou Miller,
Roger Weeks, Catherine Drew, APFEL, Sarah Entwistle,
Marlowe, Leni and Jonny Broomberg, and Fiona Jane Burgess
who inspired us to look at sign language.

First published 2015 by order
of the Tate Trustees
by Tate Publishing, a division
of Tate Enterprises Ltd,
Millbank, London SW1P 4RG
www.tate.org.uk/publishing

©Adam Broomberg & Oliver Channarin 2015
This edition ©Tate Enterprises Ltd 2015
www.broombergchanarin.com

All rights reserved. No part of this book may be reprinted
or reproduced or utilised in any form or by any electronic,
mechanical or other means, now known or hereafter
invented, including photocopying and recording, or in
any information storage or retrieval system, without
permission in writing from the publishers or a licence
from the Copyright Licensing Agency Ltd, www.cla.co.uk

A catalogue record for this book is available from
the British Library.

ISBN 978 1 84976 367 7

"When I grow up I want to be a little boy"
Joseph Heller